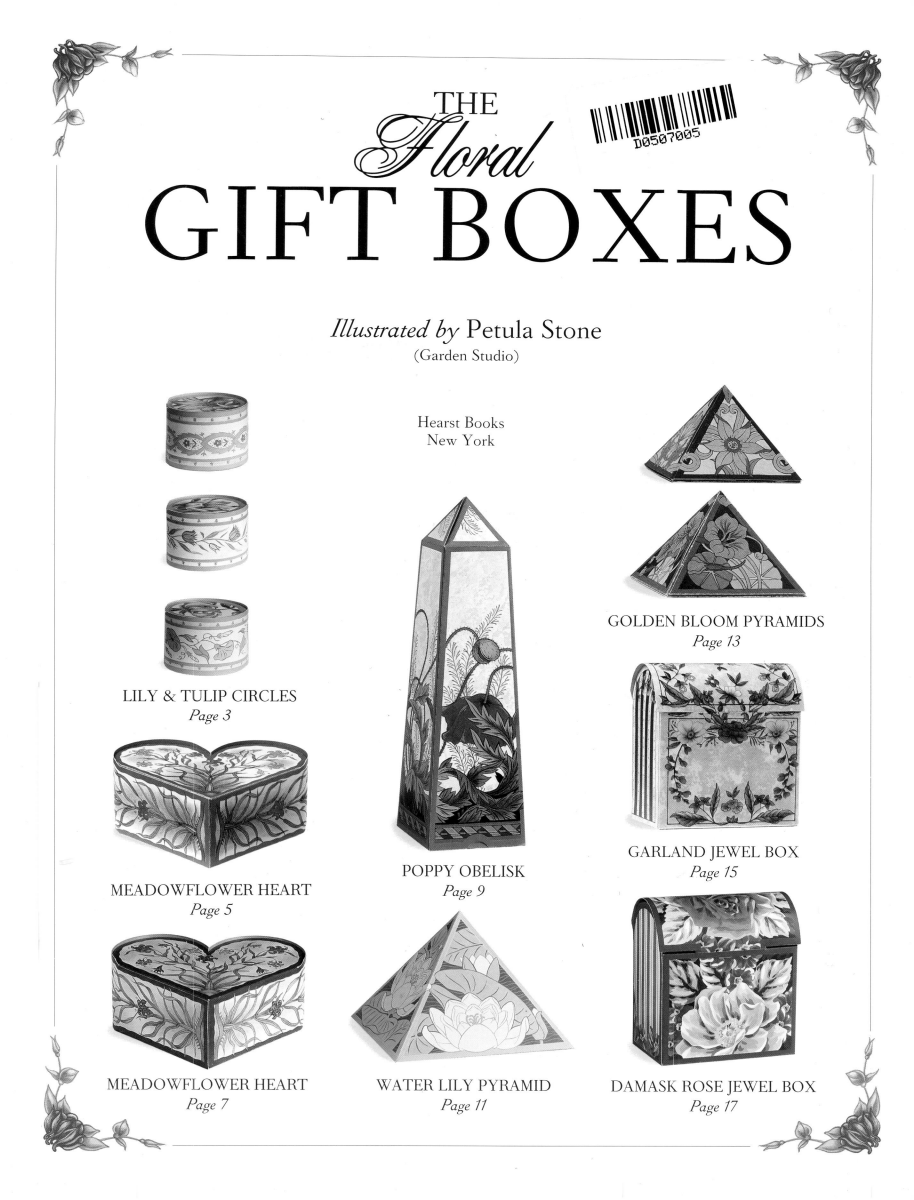

# THE *Floral* GIFT BOXES

Illustrated by Petula Stone

(Garden Studio)

Hearst Books
New York

**LILY & TULIP CIRCLES**
*Page 3*

**MEADOWFLOWER HEART**
*Page 5*

**MEADOWFLOWER HEART**
*Page 7*

**POPPY OBELISK**
*Page 9*

**WATER LILY PYRAMID**
*Page 11*

**GOLDEN BLOOM PYRAMIDS**
*Page 13*

**GARLAND JEWEL BOX**
*Page 15*

**DAMASK ROSE JEWEL BOX**
*Page 17*

**DK**

## A DORLING KINDERSLEY BOOK

Published in the United States of America in 1992 by William Morrow and Company Inc., 1350 Avenue of the Americas, New York, N.Y. 10019.

First published in Great Britain in 1992 by Dorling Kindersley Limited, 9 Henrietta Street, London WC2E 8PS, England.

*Managing art editor*
Carole Ash

*Editor*
Rosie Ford

*Art editor*
Sarah Ponder

*Production manager*
Maryann Rogers

*Paper engineer*
Chris Dartnell

Photography by Martin Cameron, Dave King, and the Dorling Kindersley studio.

Recipes on page 44 from *Chocolate* copyright © 1989 Jill Norman, published by Dorling Kindersley.

ISBN: 0-688-10985-3

Printed in Singapore
First U.S. edition
1  2  3  4  5  6  7  8  9  10

**FRUIT & FLOWER HEXAGONS**
*Page 19*

**TWINING TENDRIL PRISM**
*Page 25*

**COLUMBINE HEXAGON**
*Page 29*

**ROSE RECTANGLE**
*Page 21*

**CHINOISERIE HALF-PYRAMIDS**
*Page 27*

**COUNTRY BOWER CUBES**
*Page 23*

Assembling the boxes
*Page 33*
Gift ideas
*Page 42*

**SUMMER HEXAGONS**
*Page 31*

# LILY & TULIP CIRCLES

Assembly
instructions
*page 33*

# MEADOWFLOWER HEART

Assembly instructions
*page 34*

# MEADOWFLOWER HEART

Assembly
instructions
*page 34*

# POPPY OBELISK

Assembly instructions
*page 35*

# WATER LILY PYRAMID

Assembly
instructions
*page 36*

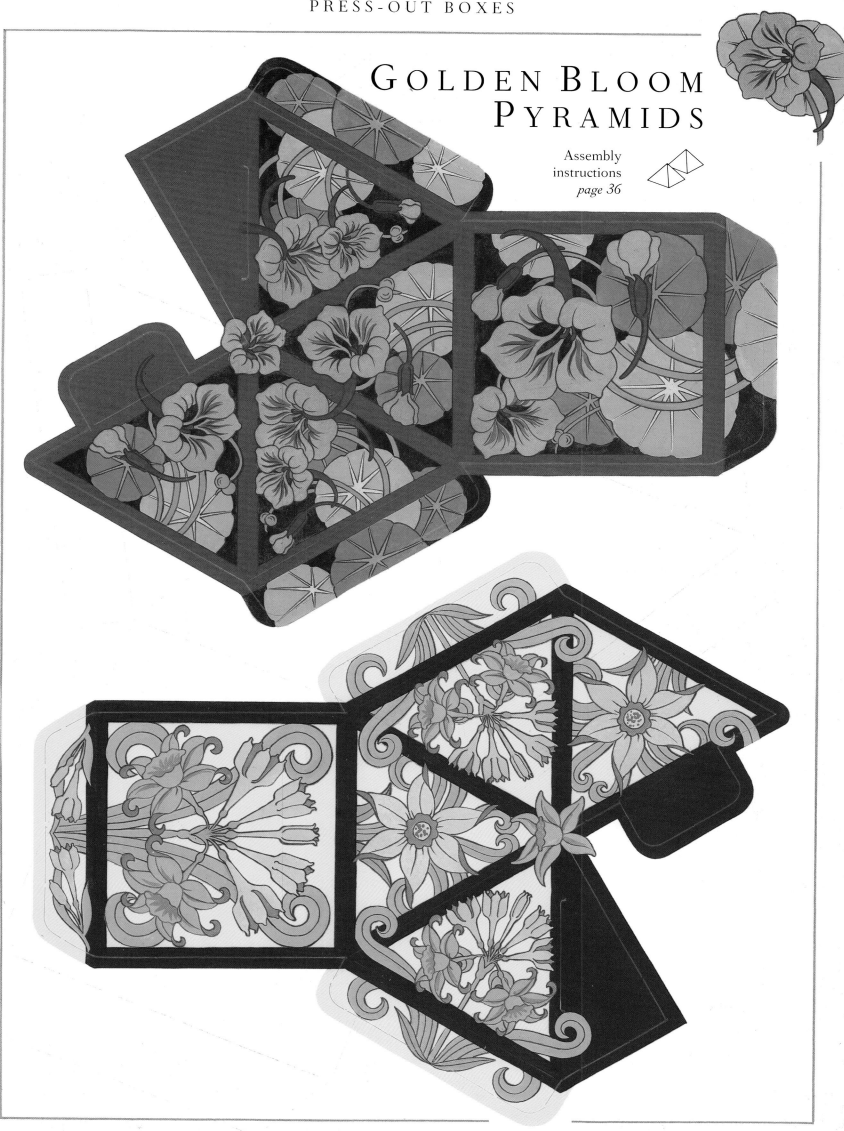

# GOLDEN BLOOM PYRAMIDS

Assembly
instructions
*page 36*

# GARLAND JEWEL BOX

Assembly instructions
*page 37*

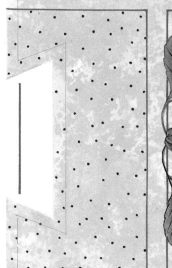
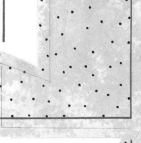

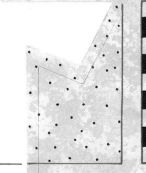
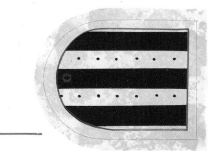

# DAMASK ROSE JEWEL BOX

Assembly instructions
*page 37*

# FRUIT & FLOWER HEXAGONS

Assembly instructions
*page 41*

# ROSE
# RECTANGLE

Assembly
instructions
*page 38*

# COUNTRY BOWER CUBES

Assembly instructions
*page 39*

# TWINING TENDRIL PRISM

Assembly
instructions
*page 40*

# CHINOISERIE
# HALF-PYRAMIDS

Assembly
instructions
*page 40*

# COLUMBINE HEXAGON

Assembly
instructions
*page 41*

# SUMMER HEXAGONS

Assembly
instructions
*page 41*

# ASSEMBLING THE BOXES

The step-by-step instructions on these pages show
how to assemble every box in the book.
Instructions are given for each shape of box and
apply to all boxes of similar shape, whatever their
dimensions. For perfect results, use a quick-drying,
clear glue, and spread it thinly on the tabs. You
will find it easier to align the sides accurately if you
use a glue that does not stick firmly on contact.
When you fold along the score lines, sharpen each
crease by pressing it with your thumb or the side
of a plastic pen. Curved surfaces need to be curled
by drawing a ruler or the blunt side of a knife blade
along the inside surface of the card.

## MAKING A CIRCLE  Press-out boxes on page 3

*Circle*
Diameter: 43 mm (1⅝ in)
Depth: 33 mm (1¼ in)

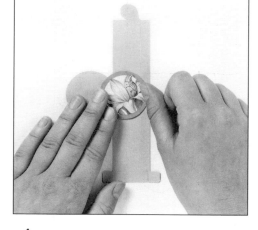

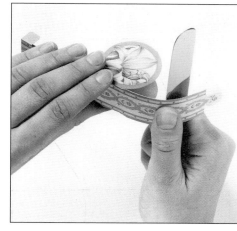

*1* *Press the box out of the page, then
place it face down and fold along the
score lines.*

*2* *Curl the two rectangular sides by
drawing a knife edge or ruler along
them (see above) to form the curved
walls of the box.*

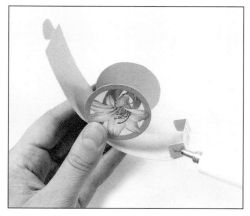

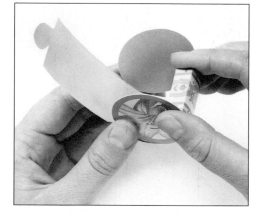

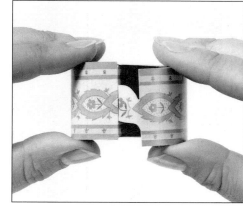

*3* *Fold the flap in and make sure
that the tabs are still bent in, then
dab a little glue on the outside of one of
the tabs.*

*4* *Stretch the side with the tabs
around the rim of the circle so that
it fits snugly. Tuck the flap in and press
the tab against the side. Dab glue on the
other tab, and repeat.*

*5* *Pull the second side around and
close the box by pushing the tongue
into the slot on the flap.*

# MAKING A HEART

Press-out boxes on pages 5 and 7

*Heart*
Top to bottom: 90 mm (3½ in)
Depth: 38 mm (1½ in)

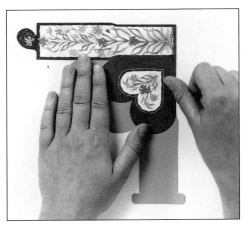

*1* Press the box out of the page, then turn it over and fold along the score lines, starting with the long ones beside the heart-shaped sides. Fold the two tiny tabs out rather than in.

*2* Turn the box over and spread glue over the two large tabs.

*3* Turn it over again, then fold up both hearts, tucking the shorter glued tab inside the longer one. Align the long tab carefully against the side and press both tabs until they stick.

*4* Curl both the long rectangular sides against the edge of a knife or ruler (see page 33).

*5* Make sure that the two tiny tabs are bent back, then dab a little glue on the outside of each one.

*6* Stretch the side with the tabs around the rim of the heart shape so that it fits snugly at the top and bottom edges.

*7* Press the tabs against the inside of the heart and hold them in place until they stick firmly.

*8* Stretch the second side around the rim of the heart, ensuring that it fits snugly at the edges. Close the box by pushing the tongue through the slot.

# MAKING AN OBELISK Press-out box on page 9

*Obelisk*
Height: 156 mm (6⅛ in)
Base: 52 mm (3¹⁄₁₆ in) square

*1* Press the box out of the page, then turn it over and fold along the score lines, starting with the long ones. Fold the top section accurately.

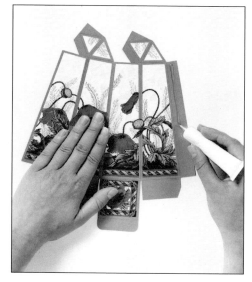

*2* Turn the box over and spread glue sparingly over the long tab at the side of the box.

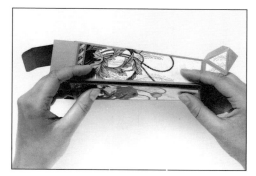

*3* Turn it over again and fold the sides around to form the body of the box. Press the glued tab against the side, aligning the edges carefully.

*4* Make sure that the sides of the box form exact right angles, then fold up the pyramid section at the top and tuck in the flaps so that you can see the shape before gluing it.

*5* Unfold the pyramid and dab a little glue on all four tabs. Fold the pyramid again, making sure that the edges are accurately aligned.

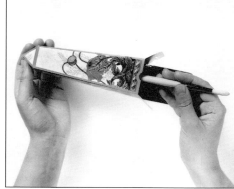

*6* Press the tabs from inside with the handle of a narrow brush or a long pencil to ensure that they stick properly.

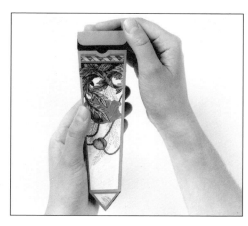

*7* Fold down the two flaps at the base, then close the box by tucking the flap into the slot.

# MAKING A PYRAMID
Press-out boxes on pages 11 and 13

*Large pyramid*
Base: 96 mm (3¾ in) square

*Small pyramid*
Base: 66 mm (2⅝ in) square

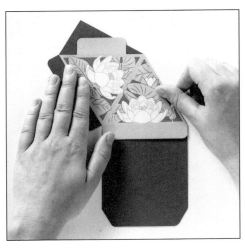

*1 Press the box out of the page, place it face down and fold along the score lines, starting with the ones radiating from the points of the triangles.*

*2 Turn the box over and spread glue sparingly on the long tab at the side of one of the triangles.*

*3 Turn the box over again and, with the square base on the table, fold up two sides to make a pyramid.*

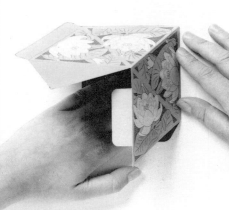

*4 Press the glued tab onto the base, aligning the edges carefully.*

*5 Spread glue on the other long tab, then fold the third triangle over and press the tab firmly against the base to form the other side of the box.*

*6 Fold up the flap at the bottom edge of the opening.*

*7 Fold the side flap over to cover half the opening.*

*8 Close the box by tucking the tab on the open side into the corresponding slot at the corner.*

# MAKING A JEWEL BOX

Press-out boxes on pages 15 and 17

*Jewel Box*
Base: 77×50 mm (3×2 in)
Height: 87 mm (3⅜ in)

*1 Press the box out of the page, then place it face down and fold along the score lines, starting with the side edges.*

*2 Turn it over and spread glue along the tab at the side edge.*

*3 Fold the sides of the box around and press the tab against the side, aligning the edges carefully. Hold it until it has stuck firmly.*

*4 Hold the box upside down and fold in the large notched flap.*

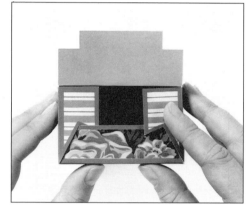

*5 Bring over one of the side flaps and push the triangular point under the notch in the first flap. Repeat with the flap on the other side.*

*6 Fold down the remaining flap and tuck the tongue into the notch on the first flap. Turn the box over and press the base gently from the inside to make it level.*

*7 Curl the outer lid over carefully by drawing it against the side of a knife or ruler (see page 33).*

*8 Fold in the inner lid, then bring the curved lid over. Slot the flap in to close the lid. If it keeps springing out, put an elastic band around the box until the lid holds its shape.*

# MAKING A RECTANGLE   Press-out box on page 21

*Rectangle*
Base: 121×60 mm (4¾×2⅜ in)
Height: 40 mm (1½ in)

**1** *Press the box out of the page, place it face down and fold along the score lines, starting with the longest ones.*

**2** *Turn the box over and spread glue sparingly over one of the tabs next to the long section that forms the back and lid of the box.*

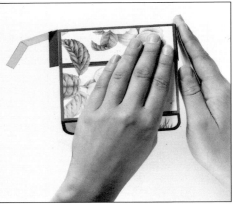

**3** *Turn the box over again and fold up the section with the glued tab. Align the corner carefully, then press the tab until it has stuck firmly. Repeat with the other tab at the back.*

**4** *Spread a little glue over one of the tabs at the front of the box.*

**5** *Fold up the front section and align the corner carefully. Press the tab until it has stuck firmly, then repeat with the remaining tab.*

**6** *Fold down the two flaps at the sides of the opening.*

**7** *Close the lid by tucking in the flap at the front.*

# MAKING A CUBE   Press-out boxes on page 23

*Cube*
All sides: 44 mm (1¾ in)

*1   Press the box out of the page, then turn it over and fold along the score lines, starting with the ones that form the side edges.*

*2   Turn it over and spread glue sparingly on the tab.*

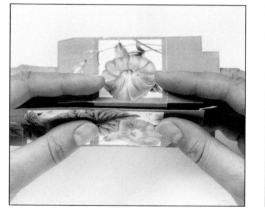

*3   Fold up the four sides of the box and, making sure that the edges are exactly aligned, stick the tab to the side and hold it in place until it has stuck firmly.*

*4   Hold the box upside down and fold in the large notched flap.*

*5   Bring over one of the side flaps and push the triangular point under the notch in the first flap. Repeat with the flap on the other side.*

*6   Fold down the remaining flap and tuck the tab into the notch on the first flap. Turn the box over and press the flaps from the inside to make sure they form a level base to the box.*

*7   Push down the two flaps at the top to cover the opening.*

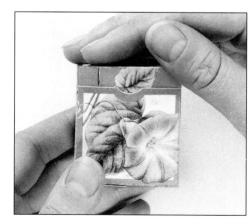

*8   Bring the lid over and slot in the front flap to close it.*

# MAKING A PRISM  Press-out box on page 25

*Prism*
Length: 150 mm (5⅞ in)
Height: 58 mm (2½ in)

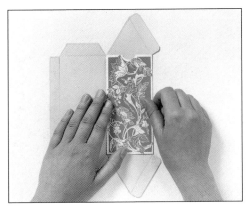

*1 Press the box out of the page, then turn it over and fold along the score lines, starting with the long ones.*

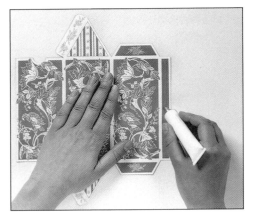

*2 Turn it over and spread glue sparingly along the tab.*

*3 Turn the box over again and fold it into a triangle. Align the edges carefully, then press the glued tab against the side, holding it in position until it has stuck firmly.*

*4 Fold in the small flap at the base, then slot in the main one. Close the lid in the same way.*

# MAKING A HALF-PYRAMID  Press-out boxes on page 27

*Half-Pyramid*
Base: 150 mm (5⅞ in)
Top: 49 mm (1⅞ in)

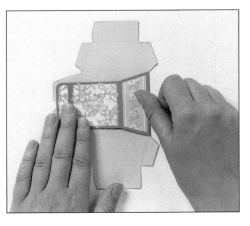

*1 Push the box out of the page, then place it face down and fold along the score lines, starting with the long ones around the square base.*

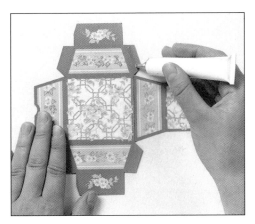

*2 Turn the box over and spread glue over one of the tabs by the long section that forms the back and lid. Turn the box over again.*

Making a half-pyramid *continued*

*3* Fold up the back and the side with the glued tab. Align the corner, then stick the tab to the back. Repeat with the other tab at the back.

*4* Fold the two flaps over the opening at the top of the box, then bring the lid down, tucking it behind the tabs at the front. Leave the front itself open.

*5* Spread a little glue on the tabs, then fold up the front. Press the front against the glued tabs and hold it until it has stuck firmly.

# MAKING A HEXAGON  Press-out boxes on pages 19, 29 and 31

*Large hexagon*
Height: 155 mm
(6⅛ in)
Diameter: 61 mm
(2⅜ in)

*Flat hexagon*
Height: 34 mm
(1⅝ in)
Diameter: 63 mm
(2½ in)

*Small hexagon*
Height: 95 mm
(3¾ in)
Diameter: 38 mm
(1½ in)

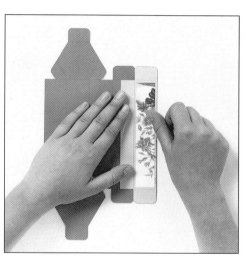

*1* Push the box out of the page, then turn it over and fold along the score lines, starting with the longest ones.

*2* Spread glue sparingly over the tab at the side.

*3* Fold the box into a hexagon, align the edges accurately and press the tab against the side.

*4* Support the box in your hand and fold in the flaps at the base.

*5* Slot in the third flap to complete the base, then close the lid by folding the flaps in the same way.

# FRAGRANT GIFTS

Everybody enjoys receiving luxuriously scented gifts; indeed perfumes and aromatic oils have been traditional offerings throughout the ages. The sweet scent of potpourri pervading a room, the refreshing tang of lavender impregnating clothes and linen, or the luxury of perfumed toiletries – whatever fragrance you choose, it can be displayed beautifully in a decorative box.

## POTPOURRI

Whether you opt for a traditional mixture of roses and cottage flowers or prefer an exotic blend of spicy fragrances, you can find potpourri to suit any taste. If you buy a ready-made mixture, give it a decorative touch of your own: a few miniature dried rosebuds add a dainty flourish to a floral potpourri, and star anise will enhance a spicy blend.

## DRIED FLOWERS

A tiny posy of dried flowers scented with essential oils will perfume the room where they are displayed.

## SCENTED CANDLES

Combining the gentle warmth of candlelight with a subtle fragrance, scented candles imbue any room with a feeling of romantic charm. Try to find candles whose color complements their scent.

## LAVENDER BAGS AND SACHETS

Perhaps the most popular of all herbal fragrances, lavender is perfect for scenting a wardrobe or linen cupboard. Make small bags of cotton or silk, fill them with dried lavender and tie the neck closed with a ribbon. Alternatively, sew two small pieces of cotton or silk together to make a sachet, trim with lace and fill with dried lavender.

# SOAP

Strongly perfumed and attractively shaped, small guest soaps make a delightful gift. If you present them on a bed of potpourri, the scent of the potpourri will impregnate the soaps to give them a heady fragrance.

# FRAGRANT TOILETRIES

Treat someone to the luxury of a perfumed bath. Bath crystals or salts will scent the bathroom as well as the bathwater, if stored in an open container. Bath pearls dissolve to give a creamy texture to the water.

# LAVENDER BATH BAGS

For an unusual gift, make tiny bags in soft cotton, muslin or fine lace and attach a loop of ribbon at the top. Fill them with a mixture of lavender heads, dried flowers, rolled oats and a little grated lemon rind. Suspended by the loop of ribbon under a running tap, the flowers and lemon scent the water, and the oats soften it.

# ESSENTIAL OILS

Perhaps the most luxurious of all perfumes, essential oils have been used for centuries for their health-giving properties as well as for their powerful scent. A selection of three or four oils makes a perfect present. They can be blended with vegetable oils to make a massage oil, or a few drops may be added to bathwater.

# PERFUME

From the fresh scent of eau-de-Cologne and sweet-smelling floral water, to the pungent fragrance of concentrated perfume, a tiny vial of scent is the ultimate indulgence. An ornate bottle adds to the luxury.

# DRAWER FRESHENERS

Sandalwood drawer fresheners give off a spicy fragrance which will impregnate the clothes or linen they are stored with. Drawer fresheners made from other woods may be scented with aromatic oils.

# EDIBLE TREATS

At Easter, Christmas, Valentine's Day, or on any special occasion, a selection of delicious chocolates, tempting cookies or mouthwatering fudge is an irresistible treat. Make your gift a visual delight by adding exquisite garnishes and decorations.

## CHOCOLATES

Indulge a chocolate-lover with a box of handmade chocolates. Introduce variety into your assortment by coating some in chopped nuts or dusting them with cocoa powder or superfine sugar. Pack them in individual paper cases or wrap them in decorative silver paper. The recipes here make about 30 chocolates.

### BRANDY AND RAISIN NUGGETS

*1/4 cup (2oz.) blanched almonds*     *1/4 cup (2oz.) dried apricots*
*1/4 cup (2oz.) skinned hazelnuts*     *4 tablespoons brandy*
*1/3 cup (3oz.) raisins*     *5 ounces chocolate*

Chop the nuts, raisins and dried apricots together finely, then stir in the brandy. Melt the chocolate in a bowl over hot water. When it is smooth, add the nut mixture and blend thoroughly. Let it cool slightly, then drop teaspoonfuls onto a sheet of foil or grease-proof paper. Leave them in a cool place for about two hours to harden.

### RUM TRUFFLES

*8 ounces semisweet chocolate*     *2 tablespoons superfine sugar*
*1/4 cup (2oz.) double cream*     *2 egg yolks*
*6 tablespoons softened butter*     *2 tablespoons rum*
*1/4 cup (2oz.) cocoa*

Melt the chocolate with a tablespoon of water in a bowl over hot water. Stir in the cream, sugar and butter, a little at a time. Let the mixture cool slightly, then add the egg yolks and rum, and beat until smooth and shiny. Let sit until cool enough to handle. Roll portions into small balls and dip each one in cocoa to coat it. Store the truffles in the refrigerator: they will keep for two to three days.

## DIPPED FRUIT AND NUTS

Cherries, candied orange peel and Brazil nuts are the most popular centers for dipping in chocolate, but you can coat almost any nut or small fruit – grapes, strawberries, almonds and dried apricots work well, too.

# COOKIES

A box of homemade cookies makes a delicious treat. When you pack them, put grease-proof paper at the bottom of the box and between each layer of cookies.

## BROWNIES

½ cup (1 stick) butter
2 x 1-ounce squares unsweetened chocolate
1 cup sugar

2 eggs
1 teaspoon vanilla
½ cup all-purpose flour
½ cup coarsely chopped nuts (optional)

Preheat the oven to 350°F. Butter and flour an 8 x 8-inch baking pan. In a heavy saucepan, melt the butter and chocolate together. Add the sugar and mix well. Remove from heat and cool for 5 minutes. Add 1 egg at a time, beating well after each addition. Add the vanilla, flour and nuts, beating well. Pour into the prepared pan and bake for 15 to 20 minutes, or until a toothpick inserted into the middle of the batter comes out clean. Cool the brownies completely before cutting into 2-inch squares. Makes 32 brownies.

## CRESCENTS

1 cup (2 sticks) butter
½ cup sugar
2 cups all-purpose flour

1 cup finely ground nuts (walnuts, almonds or pecans)
Confectioner's sugar

Preheat the oven to 275°F. In a bowl, cream the butter and sugar. Add the nuts and mix well. Add the flour gradually. Using your hands, shape approximately 1 heaping teaspoon of dough into a 1-inch crescent. Place the cookies 1 inch apart on ungreased cookies sheets. Bake for 45 minutes, or until lightly browned. Remove the cookies to wire rack and while still warm roll in confectioner's sugar. Makes 24 cookies.

# CONFECTIONERY

Bought or homemade fudge, brightly colored jelly beans, or delicately flavored sugared almonds will look delightful displayed in a decorative gift box. Pack soft or sticky sweets in individual paper cases or wrap in colored paper or foil.

# MARZIPAN FRUIT

Made simply by dyeing marzipan with a tiny amount of food coloring and shaping by hand, a box of miniature marzipan fruits makes a delightful present. For a textured effect for strawberries and citrus fruits roll them gently against a fine grater. As a finishing touch, cut silvers of green marzipan for leaves and stalks.

# SHOPPING SUGGESTIONS

Whatever gift you are searching for, whether something purely decorative or eminently practical, a valuable collectible or some inexpensive trivia, it will take on an air of glamour and luxury when presented in a decorative box. Avoid putting anything very heavy in the boxes, and protect a very small or fragile gift by packing it carefully with some attractive lining (*see page 48*).

## JEWELERY

Small but intricately decorated jewelery complements these boxes perfectly. Strings of beads, rings, pins and earrings are obvious choices, but cufflinks, silver charms or an antique watch fob are other options. Antique markets are exciting places to hunt for an unusual piece of jewelery.

## SHELLS

Some of nature's most beautiful creations, shells make an inexpensive but imaginative and attractive present. Choose a color scheme from a range of delicate pinks and lustrous mauves. A sea horse, a piece of coral or a tiny starfish adds an exotic touch to the display.

## BUTTONS

From delicate floral designs to glittering metallic, a set of well-chosen buttons can transform a garment and enhance a chosen style. There are many valuable and collectible buttons on the market, some ornate enough to be worn as brooches. Give a matching set of unusual buttons, or contribute to a collection by finding something unique.

## BEADS

Use your imagination when shopping for beads – combine large chunky shapes with more delicate ones, choose an ethnic style or go for sophisticated elegance. Colors and textures can complement the style. Complete the package with some earring findings, or thread and a clasp for a necklace.

# STATIONERY

An antique letter opener, an elegant fountain pen or a collection of unusual pencils make ideal presents. Try to find something decorative, to make a change from the usual utilitarian stationery.

# BEAUTY PRODUCTS

As an alternative to the ubiquitous collections of makeup and toiletries, look for an unusual handbag mirror, a set of luxurious makeup brushes or a small natural sponge.

# FASHION ACCESSORIES

A fine silk scarf, a bow tie or a stylish belt can revive any wardrobe, while clips, combs and ribbons for the hair offer an inexpensive way of creating a new look. Whoever you are buying for, whether you opt for sophisticated evening wear or indulge a taste for the frivolous, some small accessory is always a welcome gift.

# SEWING ACCESSORIES

The smallest pieces of sewing equipment are often the most collectible. Antique thimbles are a popular theme for collections, but ornate embroidery scissors or a decorative tape measure may be useful as well as attractive. Other ideas are a selection of embroidery silks in sumptuous colors or a piece of antique lace.

# COLLECTIBLES

Anything small and decorative makes a lovely gift. Look out for ornate silver spoons, a pair of tiny candlesticks or something unusual such as an antique coin holder.

# LINING THE BOXES

Add the final touch to your package by including some imaginative lining to protect your gift and add to the impact when the box is opened. Choose the color and style of your packing material to complement those of the box and the present.

## SILK SCARF

A softly folded silk scarf is the perfect background to a small piece of jewelery or a hair accessory, and adds an extra element to the gift.

## CRUMPLED TISSUE

Keep a fragile gift safe by making a nest of crumpled tissue paper. Use a double sheet roughly six times the size of your box, curl the edge underneath and crumple the tissue softly until it fits in the box. Push it down gently in the middle to form a well the right size to take your gift.

## RIBBONS

Lengths of coiled ribbon can be piled into the box to give a silky-soft lining. Arrange them in loops and tuck in any loose ends. Use several ribbons of the same color but various widths, or try mixing different colors.

## SHREDDED PAPER

Cut or tear narrow strips of tissue paper, then crumple them slightly, to form a soft bed for any gift. Try combining paper of different colors, or for a dramatic glittery effect, use metallic paper instead of tissue.

## ROSE PETALS

Make a delightfully fragrant nest for your gift by piling rose petals into the box. Remember that fresh petals will last for only a day or two before they wilt.

## WOOD SHAVINGS

From bold corkscrew curls to narrow ripples in pale colors, wood shavings make an attractive and unusual packaging material for your gift.